STICKMEN'S GUIDE TO THE OCEAN
– UNCOVERED

Thanks to the creative team:

Senior Editor: Alice Peebles
Fact checking: Kate Mitchell

Design: www.collaborate.agency

First published in Great Britain in 2016
by Hungry Tomato Ltd
PO Box 181
Edenbridge
Kent, TN8 9DP

A CIP catalogue record for this book is
available from the British Library.

ISBN 978-1-910684-47-4

Printed and bound in China

Discover more at
www.hungrytomato.com

STICKMEN'S GUIDE TO THE OCEAN
– UNCOVERED

by Catherine Chambers
Illustrated by John Paul de Quay

HUNGRY TOMATO™

Contents

6 .... Introduction

8 .... The Sunlight Zone
Coral reefs and whales

10 .... Superhighway
Fishing, shipping and drilling

12 .... The Twilight Zone
Crustaceans and squid

14 .... Exploring the Seabed
Diving and filming below

16 .... The Midnight Zone
Sharks and cuttlefish

18 .... Deep-sea Discoveries
A world of sponges

20 .... The Black Abyss
Hot vents and frilled sharks

22 .... Secrets of the Abyss
Searching for new species

24 .... The Ocean's Trenches
Earth's deepest valleys

26 .... Taking the Plunge
Technology at depth

28 .... Fantastic Ocean Facts

30 .... The Future...

31-32 .... Glossary and Index

Oceans

The Earth's oceans are vast connected bowls of dark basalt rock. They cover 72 per cent of the world and provide 70 per cent of our oxygen. These oceans filled with water that was created by gaseous clouds billowing over prehistoric Earth. Ocean crusts began to form less than 200 million years ago and now hold water at an average depth of 4,000 m (13,000 ft).

The Sunlight Zone
From the sunny surface to about 200 m (660 ft) deep - the continental shelf slopes down gently at this level

The Twilight Zone
From 200 m (660 ft) to 1,000 m (3,300 ft), with faint light - the continental slope dips deep into the ocean

The Midnight Zone
From 1,000 m (3,300 ft) to 4,000 m (13,100 ft), where creatures adapt to darkness and heavy water pressure

The Abyss
From 4,000 m (13,100 ft) to 6,000 m (19,700 ft) - the continental rise reaches gently up from the abyssal floor

The Ocean's Trenches
From 6,000 m (19,700 ft) to 11,000 m (36,100 ft), where steep-sided, narrow valleys plunge down

ORCA

The Sunlight Zone

In our oceans' top layer, sunlight flickers and filters through waters that teem with life. The sun's rays grow dimmer further down the layer. But these murkier depths are still full of brightly coloured plants and creatures.

Seaweed

Coral gardens

Dazzling corals are made of thin layers of a mineral, calcium carbonate. This mineral is deposited by coral polyps – tiny soft-bodied creatures. Even smaller plant organisms called 'zooxanthellae' live in the corals, creating their vivid colours. They use sunlight to grow, and give off oxygen needed by the corals.

Clownfish

Jellyfish

Coral

Octopus

Continental shelf

Starfish

Stingray

Weedy

Seaweeds are types of simple plants called algae, They grow and multiply using sunlight in their cells. Some are a mass of curls or long, stringy threads. Others have bulbs of jelly along their fleshy blades. The bead coralline alga's hard blades are pink or purple. They create habitats for sea creatures.

Microscopic life

Swarms of microscopic phytoplankton (plants) and zooplankton (animals) begin our oceans' food chain. A species called 'eukaryotic' phytoplankton helps to regulate climate by absorbing carbon gases.

Zooplankton

Phytoplankton

Munch, munch

This huge and rare sea mammal is a right whale. It is 15 m (50 ft) long and weighs the same as three heavy trucks. Yet this massive creature feeds on tiny shrimp-like copepods, swallowing up to 1,180 kg (2,600 lb) of them each day. It filters the copepods through two rows of comb-like plates called baleen.

Baleen

Copepods

Superhighway

The sunlight zone is a well-used highway for humans. We design gigantic vessels to transport vast quantities of goods across it, from port to distant port. We fish in it, exploit its riches and extract oil from its depths.

Let's go fishing

Nearly 90 per cent of marine life is found in the sunlight zone. This includes vast numbers of fish caught on the world's 4 million fishing vessels. These range from tiny rowing boats to massive trawlers that can freeze fish on board. Trawlers sail on the sunlight zone but often catch fish way below it.

Crane for lifting huge nets

Trawler

Rubbish islands

Islands of litter, which has been dumped or washed into the sea, float on the oceans. Plastic bags gather in a massive tangle, dragging in fishing gear, bottles, boat parts and other debris. They choke marine life and darken the waters below. As the plastics break down, they release tiny particles and toxic chemicals that enter the food chain.

On the ocean wave

The first ocean-going cargo ships were galleys. They began to sail from the Mediterranean Sea into the Atlantic Ocean in about 1280BCE. Goods could then reach northern Europe more easily than across mountainous lands. Ships got larger, and allowed for fishing in open waters.

396 m (1,300 ft)

Drill tower

Rotary table

Drill

Top ship

MSC Oscar, built in 2014, is the largest cargo ship, carrying 19,224 containers. Four football pitches could fit on its deck.

Drilling and spilling

About 1,500 drilling platforms are fixed above oil and gas deposits that lie beneath the ocean floor. Long drill bits cooled with mud are plunged down into the seabed to access the deposits. Storms and fires can threaten the platforms. In 2005, Hurricane Katrina destroyed 115 rigs, spilling oil into the ocean.

The Twilight Zone

The twilight zone's waters are cold and murky. Only a faint light reaches this ocean layer during the day, and everything appears a dark, indigo blue. Water pressure is high and there is little oxygen. Yet there is still plenty of life.

Coelacanth, once thought to be extinct

Continental slope

Armed nylon shrimp

Purple sea urchin

Cushion sea star

Scavengers

Many creatures in the twilight zone are scavengers. This means they feed on pieces of dead algae and fish matter that sink down from the sunlight zone above. The sunlight zone is so rich in life that the twilight creatures flourish on a feast of debris.

Continental slope

Here, the seabed angles steeply down from the continental shelf. This is called the continental slope. Sea creatures cling to or crawl along it.

Shells and spines

Crustaceans such as crab and shrimp species have hard, flexible exoskeletons protecting their bodies. Some scuttle along the seabed, chasing their prey. Others filter plankton and bacteria from the water. The spiny purple sea urchin uses its tentacle suckers, or tube feet, to breathe, move and feed.

Squid hunt

Huge sperm whales dive down over 900 m (3,000 ft) through this layer to hunt for giant squid below. These whales find their prey through echolocation, making loud clicking sounds that hit the squid and bounce back to them. This tells the whales where the giant squid are.

Whale sends and receives sound

Attaching equipment to monitor whale sound

Glowing bacteria

Spark in the dark

Many creatures in these dark depths make their own blue-green or red bioluminescent light to attract prey or a mate. The female anglerfish extends the spine of her back fin above her head, like a fishing rod. At the end, a light made of glowing bacteria lures her prey.

Carbon sinks

Scientists lower instruments to measure the amount of carbon dioxide in the oceans. Too much carbon in the atmosphere contributes to climate change. But some ocean organisms absorb carbon dioxide, removing it from the atmosphere. The microscopic copepod excretes its carbon-trapped waste, which sinks to the oceans' depths.

PELAGRA trap for catching sediment

Marine Snow Catcher for collecting water with biological debris

Breakthrough film

Filming in the twilight zone is difficult, but in 2013 a Japanese crew took the first-ever images of a giant squid. A team of three carried out 100 or so missions in a submersible to capture the 3-m (10-ft) cephalopod. They followed it down to over 900 m (2,900 ft).

The pressure at such depths is so huge and the territory so unknown, that the crew filmed from inside the three-man Triton submersible.

The giant squid's eyeball is the size of a dinner plate

Exploring the Seabed

The twilight zone is a very exciting place for oceanography, the study of our oceans. Scientists observe sea creatures, from micro-organisms to the giant squid, and watch for signs of climate change on Earth.

Tectonic plate

Hardening crust

Seafloor spreading

Rising magma

Mid-ocean ridge

From parts of the twilight zone to deep on the ocean floor, ridges of crusty rock lie on the edges of two great slabs of seabed. These are tectonic plates that spread apart, allowing hot magma beneath to rise. Here the water cools the magma to form crusty toppings. This mid-ocean ridge was not explored until 1973.

The first explorers

In 1934, scientist William Beebe (1877–1962) joined engineer Otis Barton (1899–1992) in Barton's bathysphere. The two Americans were the first to reach the twilight zone.

Oxygen supply line

180-kg (400-lb) door

Oxygen supply

Two-way communication system

Waterjet thrusters

Footpad controls

Rotary joints

Deep-sea diving

Divers need very strong suits to withstand high pressure at this level. The Exosuit (left) allows divers to plunge 300 m (1,000 ft) below the surface. It can resist high pressure even at its weakest joints. An operator at the surface monitors conditions in the Exosuit through inbuilt links, and can manoeuvre the suit, and the diver, away from danger.

The Midnight Zone

The chilly midnight zone occupies up to 90 per cent of our oceans. The only natural light here in the deep is made by bioluminescent life forms. Many creatures are black or red to hide in the near total darkness, and some have very large eyes – or no eyes at all.

Walking cucumbers

Sea cucumbers are echinoderms, which means they have spiny skins. They feed on debris floating in the sea or buried in the sand. Sea cucumbers move around on rows of tube feet with suckers. Some eject a tangle of threads, toxins or even their own internal organs to put off predators.

Cuttlefish

Blobfish

Sea cucumbers

Jelly or fish?

The jelly-like blobfish floats just above the ocean floor in Australia's deep waters. It has almost no muscle so cannot swim. It feeds by keeping its mouth open to take in small pieces of food debris. No one has yet seen a blobfish that is more than 30.48 cm (12 in) long.

Curved teeth leave wounds in a cookie-cutter shape

Shiny shark

The cookie-cutter shark is a fast swimmer that can descend to 3,700 m (12,000 ft). It shines with a bright green bioluminescence made by photophore organs that emit light. This small shark grows 50 cm (20 in) long at most, but its razor-sharp teeth bite chunks out of much larger prey, leaving cookie-cutter marks on their flesh.

Suckers and ink

The soft-bodied cuttlefish aggressively catches prey with sucker pads at the ends of its two tentacles. With these, it pushes fish and crustaceans into its sharp beak. The cuttlefish changes colour to camouflage itself. It squirts dark ink at predators and flashes bright colours during fights.

Two tentacles

Gas-filled bone

Beak

Ink sac

Eight arms near the mouth

Deep-sea Discoveries

The life forms of the midnight zone are continually under investigation. Scientists lower special traps that delicately lift up tender creatures without damaging them. They also observe microscopic organisms that feed and breathe by chemosynthesis: absorbing chemicals from the water.

Softly, softly

Sponges are soft creatures made of hundreds of special cells that help them survive. They have no internal organs. Some are scavengers, while others are predators. Once, humans harvested them to use in the bath. Now researchers study some of the 8,500 or so species to discover more about evolution.

Sponges stick to rock or move 1 mm (0.04 in) per day

Sponge medicine

Scientists study deep-sea sponges to find new treatments and cures for diseases. Some sponges contain chemicals that are being developed into medicines to fight infections. One deep-water species, *Discodermia dissoluta*, is of special interest. It may have properties that reduce some cancerous tumours.

Cells for research growing in a petri dish

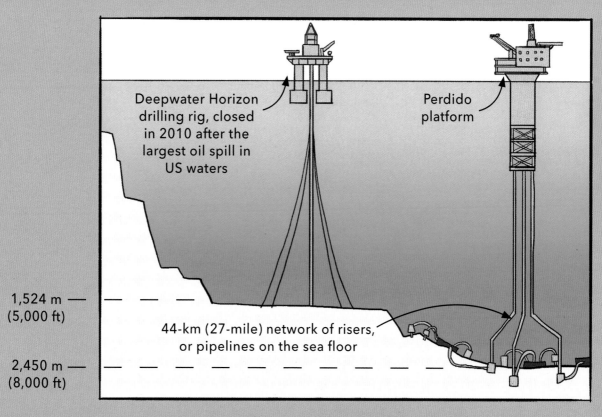

Deepwater Horizon drilling rig, closed in 2010 after the largest oil spill in US waters

Perdido platform

1,524 m (5,000 ft)

2,450 m (8,000 ft)

44-km (27-mile) network of risers, or pipelines on the sea floor

Deepest well

In the Gulf of Mexico, Perdido platform sits in 2,450 m (8,000 ft) of water above the deepest oil and gas well, which was drilled 3 km (1.9 miles) into the seabed. Perdido means 'lost' in Spanish!

Photo shoot

Remote-control cameras that withstand enormous water pressure capture images of coral gardens. Corals are important habitats for other life forms and can be indicators of climate change. More than 4,800 coral species have been found so far, over half of these in the deep sea. Some are as tiny as a small seed, while others grow as tall as a house.

Corals

Strong camera cage

Temperature:
50°C–400°C
(122°F–752°F)

Smoking chimneys

Hydrothermal vents form on the ocean floor above hot moving magma. Cracks in the floor allow seawater to seep in. This water is heated by the magma and bubbles up again. The boiling water brings with it dissolved rock minerals that harden into a crust, which builds up into chimneys.

Hydrothermal plume containing oxygen, sulphur or acids

Hydrothermal vent

Chilled out

In the Gulf of Mexico and away from the warm vents, a species of polychaete worm, or bristle worm, lives in chilly methane ice-burrows.

Polychaete worm with bristly body segments

The Black Abyss

The abyss is mostly a pitch black, icy zone, but life still exists here. And where the ocean floor lies close to inner Earth's hot magma, hydrothermal vents occur. Discovered only in 1977, these vents teem with creatures that, amazingly, survive the most hostile conditions.

Frilly gill slits

Frilled shark

The frilled shark is rarely seen but we know that its eel-like body is about 1.8 m (6 ft) long. It catches prey half its size with 300 needle-like teeth. It is named after the six frill-like gill slits at the sides of its head through which it receives oxygen.

Dead vent

Stalked jellyfish

See-through creatures

Translucent stalked jellyfish, or 'stauromedusae', live mostly near the shore, but new species have been found clustering around dead hydrothermal vents. Stalked jellyfish move very slowly, just shifting their position slightly. They are hard to spot as their colour is adapted to blend in with their habitat.

Tube worm's blood gives it a red colour

Giant tube worms

These bright red translucent creatures live around the chimneys of warm hydrothermal vents. They have no eyes, mouth or stomach. Tube worms use energy passed down by bacteria that live on them. The bacteria take in the chemical hydrogen sulphide from the vent, and this keeps the tube worms alive. In turn the bacteria live on blood produced by the tube worms.

Secrets of the Abyss

To explore the abyss, scientists use state-of-the-art technology to map its hidden crevices, monitor important global currents and look for new marine species. The discovery of hydrothermal vents (see pages 20–21) also revealed deposits of precious minerals, such as cobalt and gold.

GPS satellite

Gulf of Mexico

This is a hotspot for scientific research because of its rich deep-sea habitats, from coral mounds and glades to salty pools and expanses of mud.

Hydrophone for measuring sound

Echo sounder bouncing beams

Mapping the floor

Oceanographers survey the seabed first by using Global Positioning System (GPS) and official coast guard co-ordinates to record the position. Echo-sounding equipment profiles the undulating ocean floor. Digital hydrophones convert sounds into electrical energy, which can be measured at the surface.

Reflected sound waves

Underwater robotics

Robotic submarines, which are controlled from the surface, explore and record conditions in the abyss. Some grab samples to bring up for research. Others use fibre-optic technology to capture 3D videos and still images. Microphones pick up such sounds as whale song and volcanic eruptions on the ocean floor.

Boom arms for grabbers and instruments

Currents

Oceanographers observe deep-sea currents closely, as their movement, temperature and salt content give clues to climate change. The Antarctic Circumpolar Current begins with freezing, dense salty water sinking, kick-starting movement in this zone. It meets and mixes with warmer water and flows to other regions.

Coastal sea ice

Cold Antarctic water

Warm subtropical water

Cold salty water sinking

Useful venom

Scientists are looking ever deeper for new species that may have unexpected benefits for humans. The cone snail's lethal venom contains a wide range of chemicals that are being developed into medicines, including painkillers. The creature's powerful poison is unleashed through a long tongue called a proboscis.

Proboscis with venom

The Ocean's Trenches

Ocean floors rise and fall with the Earth's highest mountains and deepest valleys, or trenches. These can plunge 8-10 km (5-6 miles) down and are slightly warmer than the abyss above. Their habitats are rocky, though soft sediment lies at the base of some trenches.

No buoyancy swim bladder

Translucent fish

V-shaped trench

Trench formation

Most trenches are V-shaped and are formed where one oceanic plate slides beneath another. Volcanic islands often lie around a trench's rim.

Under pressure

Water pressure in the trenches is extreme. The gas-filled swim bladder that gives a fish buoyancy is not present in many deep-sea species. Instead these fish produce heavy concentrations of a chemical that helps the body's cells withstand pressure.

Volcanoes

Strings of underwater volcanoes run for miles on the deep-ocean floor. In 2011, sonar images captured the Tonga Trench as it swallowed giant volcanoes into its depths. This trench is an active fault line that runs north of New Zealand towards the small islands of Tonga and Samoa in the South Pacific Ocean. It reaches 10.9 km (6.7 miles) down at its deepest.

Trench fish

Delicate, translucent snailfish survive the depths of the trenches. In 2014, a new species was discovered 8 km (5 miles) down in the Mariana Trench. This snailfish's head is dog-shaped and its fins are very broad. Scientists believe the sensors that cover the fins detect prey in the soft mud.

Snailfish with broad fins

Mariana Trench

North America

Atlantic Ocean

Europe

Asia

Africa

Pacific Ocean

Pacific Ocean

South America

Australia

Indian Ocean

Deep, deeper...

The Mariana Trench is the deepest in our oceans. Its lowest point is the Challenger Deep, 10.99 km (6.83 miles) down. In 2005, scientists examined samples from its soils. They were surprised to find the single-celled 'foraminifera' organism, which has a soft shell, living so deep down. It is normally found in the layers above.

Taking the Plunge

The trenches are an exciting wilderness for scientists to explore, but conditions are tough. Equipment has to cope with a weight of water almost as heavy as 50 jumbo jets. Research has to be carefully managed so that habitats are not destroyed.

Deepsea Challenger

Stabilizer fin

2.4-m (8-ft) light panel

Battery panel

Boom arms for lights and cameras

Pilot 'ball' – operational cabin

Deepsea Challenger

In 2012, film-maker James Cameron piloted the Australian-built *Deepsea Challenger* submersible to the Challenger Deep, at the bottom of the Mariana Trench. This vehicle carries 3D cameras and sampling instruments. Its body is made from Isofloat, a foam that can withstand extreme pressure. Within the pilot's sphere, the pressure does not change.

Mapping the trenches

Echo sounding maps the shape of our deeply plunging seabed. Echo sounders work by reflecting sound waves off the bottom. The waves' lengths show the rise and fall of the ocean floor. Echo sounding was first used in 1920 by German physicist Alexander Behm (1880-1952).

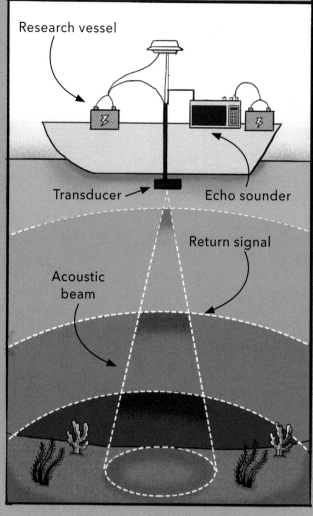

Research vessel

Transducer

Echo sounder

Return signal

Acoustic beam

ORCA

Infrared LED illuminators

ORCA camera

Deep down this 'Eye-in-the-Sea' illuminates the image in front of it using powerful red lights that most creatures in this zone cannot see.

Tracking earthquakes

The trenches help us to find ways of monitoring earth tremors. Hydrophone instruments (example right) are lowered into the trench. These measure the pressure from any movement in the trench floor. The hydrophones' transponders (the yellow spheres) convert the movements into electrical signals that are analysed at the surface.

Transponder

Fantastic Ocean Facts

Great Pacific garbage patches

Plastic litter 'islands' cover an amazing 5,000 km² (1,931 sq miles) of the Pacific Ocean. The islands are not solid, consisting mostly of small plastic pieces and microplastics. The two largest islands are the Western Pacific Garbage Patch towards Japan, and the Eastern Pacific Garbage Patch towards California.

Toxic algae

About 40 out of 4,000 species of microscopic phytoplankton algae are highly poisonous, killing millions of fish and shellfish! In recent decades they have grown into huge floating red blankets, called blooms. In 2015, a giant floating bloom was seen stretching from the central California coast all the way to Washington State, USA.

Dense underwater forests

Giant kelp is a variety of seaweed that forms thick underwater forests. This towering brown alga can grow up to 46 cm (18 in) each day, and reach a height of 53 m (175 ft). Air bladders help its dense canopy to float on top of the water, sheltering thousands of fish and shellfish species, and even seals and whales.

Colossal coral reef

Off the east coast of Australia lies the largest living structure on Earth, the Great Barrier Reef. This mass of 600 hard and soft corals stretches around 2,300 km (1,430 miles) and covers 344,400 km² (132,970 sq miles). Its different habitats provide perfect conditions for 1,625 varieties of fish, 3,000 of molluscs, 133 shark species, and many more.

Deep-sea archaeology

Digging for history can take place on the ocean floor! Here, marine archaeologists find sunken artefacts – and occasionally, treasure. In 350BCE, a heavily laden Ancient Greek cargo ship sank in the Aegean Sea. About 2,350 years later, a robot detected its cargo of elegant jars, or amphorae, containing… olive oil!

Shark shocks

Sharks were around 200 million years before dinosaurs! So they've had plenty of time to evolve into more than 465 species. They range in size from the tiny spined pigmy shark at 18 cm (7 in), to the 15-m (50-ft) whale shark. They use their nostrils solely for smelling, which is why some species can detect one part of blood in a million of water!

Super starfish

Starfish, or sea stars, have five arms each but they don't worry if they lose a few, as they just grow more! Each arm has an eye at the end of it, which can detect light, dark and basic shapes. Starfish have no brains or blood. They can feel, though, because they have a nervous system that spreads through their arms.

Tallest mountain

The highest mountain on land is Mt Everest, at 8,850 m (29,035 ft). But the tallest mountain from the base to the summit is Mauna Kea, which rises 10,200 m (33,465 ft) from the bottom of the Pacific Ocean. On land, its peak reaches 4,205 m (13,796 ft) above sea level. Mauna Kea is an inactive volcano and formed over one million years ago.

The Future...

We know less about vast areas of our oceans than about any other habitat on Earth. We do know that they hold precious resources and treatments for diseases. But our oceans need care.

Climate change

Our climate has warmed fast over the last 200 years. Most scientists believe that burning fossil fuels has caused this by releasing too much carbon dioxide into the air. Carbon gases absorb warmth, which cannot escape into the upper atmosphere. Instead, it is reflected back onto Earth. The rise in temperature affects ocean layers.

Rising seas

A warming climate makes sea levels rise by melting ice at the poles. Higher sea levels may threaten to drown small low-lying islands, and even towns and cities along continental coastlines. A warmer climate also increases the strength of cyclones and the damaging effects of waves.

Overfishing

Fishing fleets trawl with huge nets in the deep ocean. They have reduced fish stocks, threatened species and destroyed some deep-sea habitats. The biggest trawler ever built was *Atlantic Dawn*, at 144 m (472 ft) long. It located huge shoals of fish using sonar technology and could process and freeze 363 tonnes (400 tons) of fish every 24 hours.

Ocean clean-up

Oil spills and plastic bag islands pollute our oceans. Climate change has led to vast blankets of toxic algae floating on the surface. But new technology is helping to clean up the seas. The Ocean Cleanup Array is a 2,000-m (6,500-ft) flexible ring designed to enclose plastic waste so it can be removed. It is hoped that by 2021 it will have cleaned up half the Great Pacific Garbage Patch between Hawaii and California.

Glossary

Algae

Simple plant forms ranging from micro-algae to large seaweeds

Basalt

Volcanic rock made from quickly cooled lava

Calcium carbonate

Mineral deposited by shelled creatures

Cargo

Load of transported goods

Container

Metal box used to transport goods. Most are 6 m (20 ft) long

Copepod

Tiny shelled crustacean

Continental shelf

Shallow underwater shelf that extends from continents into oceans

Echinoderm

Family of underwater creatures, many with spines or raised blobs on their bodies

Erode

To wear away by natural action such as wind, water and waves

Food chain

A sequence of life forms, each one dependent on the next as a food source in order to survive

Hydrothermal

Changing boiling liquids into hard crystals

Plankton

Tiny organisms, such as bacteria, plants and shellfish, that drift in colonies because they are too weak to swim

Styrofoam

Spongey polystyrene board

Submersible

Equipment that can work or travel underwater

Swim bladder

Gas-filled pouch inside a fish that stops its body from sinking in the water

Toxin

Poison created inside living cells or organisms

Translucent

Allowing light to filter through

Venom

Toxin injected into prey or an enemy predator

Zooxanthellae

Tiny organisms living on larger life forms that depend on them for survival

INDEX

A
abyss 6, 20-23
anglerfish 13

B
bioluminescent light 13, 16, 17
blobfish 16
bristle worms 20

C
carbon sinks 14
cargo ships 11
climate change 30
cone snails 23
continental slope 12
coral 8, 19, 28
crustaceans 12
currents 23
cuttlefish 17

D
deep-sea archaeology 29
deep-sea diving 15
Deepsea Challenger 26

E
echo sounding 22, 27
echolocation 13
explorers 15

F
filming underwater 14, 19, 26
fishing 10, 30

G
giant squid 13, 14
Gulf of Mexico 19, 20, 22

H
hydrophones 22, 27
hydrothermal vents 20, 22

M
mapping 27
Mauna Kea 29
Mariana Trench 25
medicines 18, 23
midnight zone 6, 16-19

O
oceanography 15, 22, 23
oil 11, 19
ORCA cameras 27

P
phytoplankton 9
plastic rubbish 10, 28, 30

R
robotic submarines 23

S
sea cucumbers 16
sea levels 30
seaweeds 8, 28
sharks 17, 21, 29
snailfish 25
sponges 18
stalked jellyfish 21
starfish 29
sunlight zone 6, 8-11

T
toxic algae 28, 30
trenches 6, 24-27
tube worms 21
twilight zone 6, 12-15

V
volcanoes 25, 29

W
whales 9, 13

Z
zooplankton 9

The Author

Catherine Chambers was born in Adelaide, South Australia, grew up in the UK, and studied African History and Swahili at the School of Oriental and African Studies in London. She has written about 130 books for children and young adults, and enjoys seeking out intriguing facts for her non-fiction titles, which cover history, cultures, faiths, biography, geography and the environment.

The Illustrator

John Paul de Quay has a BSc in Biology from the University of Sussex, UK, and a graduate certificate in animation from the University of the West of England. He devotes his spare time to growing chilli peppers, perfecting his plan for a sustainable future and caring for a small plastic dinosaur. He has three pet squid that live in the bath, which makes drawing in ink quite economical …